helium

By Rudy Francisco

helium

POEMS BY

Rudy Francisco

——

Published by Button Poetry / Exploding Pinecone Press
Minneapolis, MN 55403 | http://www.buttonpoetry.com

——

Cover Design: Nikki Clark

ISBN 978-1-943735-19-8

Contents

I

II

III

IV

I

Water

When I was six years old,
my brother and my cousins
tried to teach me how to swim.

They did this by throwing me into a pool.
Immediately, my arms became two skinny
brown flailing distress signals.

I think I heard my brother say,
"If he dies, I'm going to be in so much trouble."
I remember them pulling me from the jaws
of the liquid beast before it could devour me whole.
That was the day I almost lost my life.

To anyone brave enough to love me,

Do you know the human body is approximately
sixty percent water? When I walk into a room
full of people, all I see is an ocean.

Good Morning

Get out of bed.
The day has been
asking about you.

It dragged the sun into your
room this morning,

pulled an entire disco of light
through your curtains,

hoping that all of this gleam
would be enough to get your attention.

This is how today says,
notice me.

Ouch

Yesterday, I injured myself
and the explanation didn't make sense.

I said, "Well, I was walking..."
and that was the end of the story.

At this age,
my body is a stranger that I
keep meeting over and over again.

The words "I am" are slowly
transforming into "I used to be"

because every year,
the past tense finds a larger house
inside the neighborhood of my
everyday vernacular.

I am slowly realizing that
when the skeleton is new
and the bones are vibrant,

they coerce the mind into
thinking the days will pass,
but the flesh will not.

Youth promises us immortality,
but doesn't have the means to
uphold its end of the bargain.

Page

It just sits there, with a mouth
full of entitlement, staring at you
and wondering why it is still
not a masterpiece.

Drive

Tell me a story
and let's laugh like it's the only
thing keeping us alive.

Play a song
and give the stereo
permission to use its
outside voice.

Let's sing loudly,
offbeat and out of tune.
Let the world know
we don't care how it sounds
because the only key we need
is already in the ignition.

Let the sky turn the windshield
into a stage. Watch it dance like the scenery
is auditioning to be a part of our story.

Let's just go.
Drive until our troubles
phantom in the rearview mirror

and we forget they exist,
at least
for a moment.

Horizon

I hope I haven't already driven
past my greatest moments.

I hope there is something
beautiful on the horizon
that's just as impatient as I am.
Something so eager,
it wants to meet me halfway.
A moment that is diligently
staring at its watch, trembling with
nervousness, frustrated,
and bursting at the seams,
wondering what's taking me
so long to arrive.

Instructions

Gather your mistakes,
rinse them with honesty
and self-reflection,

let dry until you
can see every choice
and the regret
becomes brittle,

cover the
entire surface
in forgiveness,

remind yourself
that you are human

and this too
is a gift.

My Honest Poem

I was born on July 27th. I hear
that makes me a Leo. I have
no idea what that means.

I'm 5'6
and a half,
I weigh one hundred and seventy-five pounds,

I don't know how to swim,
I'm a sucker for a girl with a nice smile
and clean sneakers. I'm still learning

how to whisper, I'm loud in places
where I should be quiet, I'm quiet
in places where I should be loud,

I was born feet first and I've been
backwards ever since. I like ginger ale.
A lot.

I've been told that I give really bad hugs.
People say it feels like I'm trying to escape.
Sometimes it's because I am.

I get really nervous every time someone
gets close enough to hear me breathe.
I have an odd fascination with sandcastles

and ice sculptures:
things that will only last a few moments.
That's also why I fall in love with women

who will never love me back.
I know it sounds crazy,
but it's actually much easier than it seems

and I think it's safer that way.
Relationships remind me that I'm not afraid
of heights or falling, but I'm afraid of what's

going to happen
when my body hits the ground.
I'm clumsy. Yesterday I tripped

over my self-esteem, landed on my pride
and it shattered like an iPhone
with a broken face. Now I can't even tell

who's trying to give me a compliment.
Sometimes, I wonder what my bedsheets say
about me when I'm not around.

I wonder what the curtains would do
if they found out about all the things
I've done behind their backs.

I've got a hamper full of really loud mistakes
and a graveyard in my closet.
I'm afraid if I let you see my skeletons,

you'll grind the bones into powder
and get high on my fault lines.
I've never been in the military,

but I have a purple heart:
I got it from beating myself up
over things that I can't fix.

Some days I forget that my skin
is not a panic room.

Hi. My name is Rudy.
I enjoy frozen yogurt,
people-watching, and laughing

for absolutely no reason at all,
but I don't allow myself to cry
as often as I need to.

I have solar-powered confidence
and a battery-operated smile.
My hobbies include: editing my life story,

hiding behind metaphors,
and trying to convince my shadow
that I'm someone worth following.

I don't know much,
but I do know this:
Heaven is full of music,

and God listens to my heartbeat
on his iPod. It reminds him
that we still got work to do.

Machine

I cannot fix you.
I can only show you
how I use the wrench,

how I turn the bolts,
how I put mistakes
inside a belt and make
them tools,

how I look the
machine in the face,

call it unfinished,
call it beautiful
and give it
my name.

Correctly

I want you to bite my lip until I can no longer speak and then suck my ex-girlfriend's name out of my mouth just to make sure she never comes up in our conversations. I want you to come to me like an afternoon, come to me slowly as if you were a broken sunset with a lazy sky on your shoulders. If you let me be your sunlight, I promise I will penetrate your darkness until you speak in angel wings. Pull me close to you, tell me that you love me, and then scratch your future into my back so I can be everything you live for. I promise I will love you as if it's the only thing I've ever done correctly.

12 am

I don't know if I can call this love.

What I do know is that my mind
is a freeway that is too familiar
with rush hour and thinks bumper-
to-bumper traffic is normal.

However, she makes everything
feel like midnight.

The streets are empty and her car
is the only one on the road.

Sip

I take my compliments
the same way I take
my coffee.

I don't drink coffee.

The last time I did,
it seared my entire mouth
and I couldn't taste
anything for three days.

I'm still learning how to
let endearment sit until
it's ready to be consumed,

hold it to my lips
and sip slowly.

Petal

The tongue has a jagged beauty
and I know how easily the mouth
can become a rose bush.

To the Girl Who Works at Starbucks, Down the Street from My House on Del Mar Heights Road, I Swear to God I'm Not a Stalker

When I asked you for a chai latte,
what I meant to say was:
"I was walking past. I saw you in the window.
I only came in here because I had to know
what your voice sounded like."

But instead of saying that, I got really nervous
and just ordered the first thing on the menu.
I don't even know what "chai" is.

Or a latte, for that matter.

I imagine, when God made you,
he cussed for the first time. He turned to an angel,
gave him a high five and said: "Goddamn, I'm good!"
You are that beautiful. I spent the last five days
trying to figure out how I'm going to introduce myself
to you properly, and I think I've finally figured it out.
It's going to be something like..."Hi."

That's all I got so far, but I think it's a good start.

Alternatives to "Bae"

The one who wins all of the arguments,
the keeper of the remote, the girl who
turns my stomach into a butterfly nest,
the pink Starburst, the one I will always
choose first no matter what else is in the
pack, the red Kool-Aid, the right amount
of sugar, the pulp, the part that makes
the juice seem real.

If I Was a Love Poet

I'll be honest; I'm usually not really a love poet.
In fact, every time I try to write about love, my hands cramp
just to show me how painful love can be and sometimes,
pencils break just to prove that every now and then,
love takes a little more work than planned.
I'm not much of a love poet. But if I was to wake up
tomorrow morning and decide that I really wanted
to write about love, my first poem would be about you. About how
I loved you the same way that I learned how to ride a bike.
Scared, but reckless. With no training wheels or elbow pads
so my scars can tell the story of how I fell for you.

I'm not much of a love poet, but if I was, I'd write about how I see
your face in every cloud and your reflection in every window. I've
written a million poems, hoping that somehow, you'll jump out of
the page and be closer to me. Because if you were here right now,
I would massage your back until your skin sings songs
that your lips don't even know the words to.
Until your heartbeat sounds like my last name.
And you smile like the Pacific Ocean.
I want to drink the sunlight in your skin.

If I was a love poet, I'd write about how
you have the audacity to be beautiful
even on days when everything around you is ugly.
I'd write about your eyelashes, and how they are like
violin strings that play symphonies every time you blink.

If I was a love poet, I'd write about how I melt in front of you
like an ice sculpture every time I hear the vibration in your voice
and whenever I see your name on the caller ID, my heart plays

hopscotch inside of my chest. It climbs onto my ribs
like monkey bars and I feel like a child all over again.

I know this is going to sound weird, but sometimes,
I pray that God somehow turns you back into one of my ribs
just so I would never have to spend an entire day without you.
I swear, I'm usually not a love poet, but if I were to wake up
tomorrow morning and decide that I really want to write about
love, my first poem would be about you.

Again

After Ainsley Burrows

Last night, I had a dream. And in this particular dream, I died in my dreams, woke not knowing I was still sleeping and decided to walk. That night, I walked in my sleep, I slept in my walk, I walked backwards until I saw you for the first time, and I could barely muster the courage to introduce myself all over again. I've been trying to find the right words. I've been trying to take the right steps for what seems to me like thousands of years, but something always seems to go wrong between us. We lived in Egypt, I was the Pharaoh's slave, you were his daughter. Loving you led to my death, they claimed I seduced you, and after they stole my life, I was resurrected as a mason. I made the foundation for your house. We met eyes for two seconds, you left, and I didn't see you again until I died. I came back as a caterpillar. I turned into a butterfly, I landed in the palm of your hands, you brushed me away, and the rejection killed me. When I awoke, I was a kick drum, you were a snare, we were both owned by this drummer named Cozy Cole, and when he died, so did we, but I came back just to look for you. I left notes in random places, hoping that you would stumble across them. I carved our names in trees, and then prayed it would jog your memory. I whispered your name in the wind, hoping somehow, maybe some way, my voice would reach you, but it didn't, and I died. I died early. I died young with breadcrumbs in my hand, so they buried me and when they buried me, they put these coins over my eyes, and I used them as bus fare to get back to Earth, just so I can look for you.

II

Sinking

I held you
the way a boat holds water.

I should have left when I
felt us sinking.

When People Ask How I'm Doing

I want to say,

my depression is an angry deity, a jealous god
a thirsty shadow that wrings my joy like a dishrag
and makes juice out of my smile.

I want to say,

getting out of bed has become a magic trick.
I am probably the worst magician I know.

I want to say,

this sadness is the only clean shirt I have left
and my washing machine has been broken for months,

but I'd rather not ruin someone's day with my tragic honesty
so instead I treat my face like a pumpkin.

I pretend that it's Halloween.
I carve it into something acceptable.
I laugh and I say,

"I'm doing alright."

Mess

On the day you couldn't hold yourself together anymore,
you called for me, voice cracking like two sets of knuckles
before an altercation.

I found you, looking like a damaged wine glass.
I hugged your shatter. I cut all of my fingers
trying to jigsaw puzzle you back together.

When it was over,
you looked at the stains on the carpet
and blamed me for making a mess.

Vanish

They will push you away, tell you
to leave, but have no idea how good
you are at following instructions.

When you vanish, but your ghost
becomes a guest they cannot get rid of

and the memory of you plays
resurrection with their smile,

they will ask where you went,
if you will come back and why
you gave up so easily,

as if they didn't own the voice
that requested your disappearance.

They now know solitude does not
scare people like us

and our absence is something
that we are not afraid to give
to those who call for it.

Why Did You Leave?

Because
you wouldn't let me
love both of us
at the same time.

Scars

1.

If I could
I would nail these hands
to the edges of stars.
I would sacrifice
this body to the sky
hoping to resurrect as someone
spiteful enough
to not care about you.

2.

Staple me to a cross.
Pierce my side with a broken promise.
I will bleed all the crippled reasons
why you deserve one more chance.

3.

Loving you
was the last thing
I felt really good at.

4.

You want to know
how I got these scars?
I ripped every last piece of you
out of my smile.

5.

I whispered you stardust.

6.

I spoke you into sunflowers.

7.

I dipped my hands in forever,
touched you infinity.
Treated you as if you were
the last molecule of oxygen
inside of a gas chamber.
I was so good to you.

8.

You want to know
how I got these scars?
I swallowed my pride.
It clawed its way
out of my mouth.

9.

I realized I was never
really your boyfriend.
I was your hype man.

10.

I hope your next boyfriend
gets smallpox.

10.

Yes, I said smallpox.

10.

I hate you.

10.

I still miss you.

10.

I still love you.

10.

I love you.

10.

I love you.

10.

It's hard for me to count
when I get emotional.

10.

I heard 90% of human
interaction is nonverbal, so...

10.

If I could
I would tie your arms to a daydream
and auction you off
to my fondest memories.
I wrote this poem in
my own spinal fluid.
I put it on the backbone of a white flag.
Before you read it
you'll already know I've given up.

I'll keep you here.
Shackled to the most important
chapter of my life story,
pressed into the
basement of my eyelids
like liquid salvation
so I remember you beautiful.
With amazing underneath your wings
and an orchid smile.

You gorgeous earthquake.

You cracked hourglass
with sand spilling from behind your ribs.
You wasted my time.

How dare you linger on my lips
and then kiss me like a stuttering apology
with excuses stapled to the roof of your mouth?

I still remember you
like a dream tattooed to the inner walls
of a long-term memory,
but some days I wonder if you existed at all.

And of course,
you want to know how I got these scars.
I'll tell you.
I got these scars
the day I fell in love with you.

I landed face-first.

Museum

No one ever asks a museum
if it's doing okay.

So when you choose to spill like this,
bleed like this, cry like this,
your pain becomes an exhibit.

You hang your trauma on the wall,
ask patrons not to touch, but only
half of them respect the signs.

When you choose to be a poet,

you become a place that people walk through
and then leave when they are ready.

To the Random Dude Who Started Dating My Ex-Girlfriend Two Days After We Broke Up (Yes, I Read That on Facebook)

When I saw that you were in a relationship with the girl that I thought I would spend the rest of my life with, I walked outside. I said to myself, "There's no way Ashton Kutcher is going to catch me off guard." I waited 45 minutes and then I realized, there hasn't been a new episode of *Punk'd* in almost three years, so I guess I'm the only practical joke in this entire situation.

One: The first time I saw you and her in a picture, I wanted to take my entire arm, shove it inside of the computer, and snatch the happiness right off of your face.

Two: If I ever see you in the street, I'm probably going to punch you in the throat.

Three: I apologize in advance. And I know that it makes no sense to have this much anger toward a man that I have never met face to face, but my definition of love is being robbed in an alley eight times in a row and hoping there's something about today that makes all of this different. There is nothing logical about cutting off the most important parts of yourself then putting them inside hands that shake, that tremble, that crack like a Haitian sidewalk.

Four: There is nothing rational about love. Love stutters when it gets nervous, love trips over its own shoelaces. Love is clumsy, and my heart refuses to wear a helmet.

Five: Cupid is irresponsible, and I'm tired of him using me for target practice.

Six: I was told that time would heal all wounds. But what exactly do you do on days when it feels like the hands on your clock have arthritis?

Seven: She always wore her heart on her sleeve. So tell me, why do you look so familiar?

Eight: I think I've seen you somewhere in her smile. I feel like I've heard your voice in her laughter. I bet if we dusted her heart for fingerprints we would only find yours.

Nine: I have this envelope. It's full of all the butterflies I felt the first time she relaxed the Velcro on her lips and smiled in my direction. I think most of them are still alive.

I suppose these belong to you, too.

Haunted

On days like this,
I am the house and
the ghost,

responsible for my
own haunting.

My brain is a revolver
with "Am I good enough?"
in every chamber.

So I turn into a factory that
only makes the word "yes"
and I say it until it can easily
be mistaken for the truth,

but my voice shakes
and the answer still sounds
like a question.

How Did You Lose Her?

I felt trapped,
but another man
looked at my prison
and called her a church.

Who would choose to be a jail
when given the option
of being a sanctuary?

Chameleon

When I was in the 5th grade I knew a kid
named Javier. He was black, which was confusing.

He was an African-American kid who spoke
Spanish, loved country music, wore cowboy

boots, played jump rope and had a look on his
face that said: I wish a motherfucker would say

something. None of us said anything. For show
and tell, he brings in his pet chameleon. When he

walks in, the eyes of every kid glaze over like the
windows to our souls shook hands with the winter

for the first time. A girl with box springs in her throat
felt the silence and it was just too heavy for her fingertips

to hold on to so she drops the quiet like a suitcase full of
habits that no one wants to keep and says, "So what's his name?"

He replies, "I call him Rudy." When the class realized that me
and the lizard had the same name, they laughed uncontrollably.

Twenty years later, the irony hits me over the head like an empty
Heineken bottle inside of the bar fight that I call my everyday life.

I get it. Chameleons have the ability to paintbrush themselves
into whatever will match their surroundings. They do it so often,

they probably wouldn't be able to recognize a photograph of their
own skin. They think it is far better to be invisible than it is to

grind their teeth into "I dare you" and to ride their bones like a
magic carpet, no steering wheel, no tires, no brakes, no battery

just bravery and a chest full of "I am not dying today."
Courage has never been a chameleon's best attribute

and some days, it's not mine either. I was mentored by black men
with brown skin who turned yellow at the sight of bellies

swollen with half their DNA. I was taught that a woman's vagina
is just an underground railroad to masculinity, that real men

have tunnel vision and treat girls like subway cars,
like nothing more than a space to parallel park our genitals,

a hole to bury seeds and leave orchards in our rear-view mirrors.
They say you have to peel a woman like a tangerine

and your job as a man is to chameleon yourself into her trees,
bite a piece of her fruit and leave the rest hanging

crooked and confused. This is an apology to every woman
I changed colors just to get inside of.

I still haven't stumbled across a definition of a man,
but I know that we are hotels that stand a million war stories tall.

I know that we carry guitar cases full of phobias
hoping we can turn fear into our strongest instrument,

I know that our hands break things just as frequent
as we can fix them. And we often forget that sexism

is a family heirloom that we've been passing down for generations. As men, it is important that we start asking ourselves,

What will the boys learn from us?

Windows and Mirrors

There was a moment in my life
when I couldn't tell the difference
between a window and a mirror.

I could look into both
and see everything
but myself.

Lopsided

She is a stuttering soliloquy. A wounded symphony played by an orchestra of her family's I-told-you-so's. A tattered woman who bleeds like an oak tree. Her life story is just a sandpaper love song written on a napkin full of all the reasons why no one should ever try to hug the rain. You always end up soaking wet and by yourself.

She has violin strings for legs, a graveyard of awkward treble clefs buried in her knees and I can see the suffering inside of the concert of her walk.

She comes over on Wednesdays. Walks into my room like a question that neither one of us has the courage to ask. Sometimes, words get too heavy to sit on the ivory pedestals that we've built inside of our mouths. Sometimes, our actions join hands and become behaviors that are too complicated for lips to say out loud, so instead, we just liberate our flesh, letting skin speak on our behalf, the language of those who are just as afraid of commitment as they are of being alone and we speak it like it's our native tongue.

Honestly, I can't tell you her favorite color, her middle name or what her face looks like during the day. All I know is that we are both allergic to the exact same things. Compliments, the word beautiful, and someone saying I love you with arms full of acceptance and sincerity on their breath.

Most days, I wonder what she carries in the luggage underneath her eyes. I wonder if those bags ever get too heavy for her face. But instead, I let those questions sandcastle inside of my stomach. I amputate the parts of me that have grown fond of her smell.

I wash my sheets and I think to myself, most men are proud of things like this.

To You

He puts guilt in the air and waits for you
to breathe, tries to tailor the blame until it
looks like it fits you, turns the story into a
gymnast and convinces it to flip. He rewinds
the movie, excavates the plot, digs out your
patience, makes himself the narrator and the
hero. He sketches you as the antagonist and
suddenly his transgressions become deleted
scenes. He blames you for his sadness.

And this is how the wolf cries boy.

To Him

I'm just sorry that
she had to be your
fortune cookie.

Broken so you could
learn a lesson

you already
should've known.

And Then After

Our last conversation
ended with yelling.

We both said things
we didn't mean.

I heard there's a
woman in Palestine
who makes flower pots
out of used teargas grenades.

From this I learned
the explosion

is not how the story
has to end.

III

Waves

There was a point in my life
when I had a matching durag
for every outfit in my closet

and today,
if you look hard enough,
you can still see the lines
on my forehead.

These are fossils from a
simpler time, ruins of an
orange can empire.

Back when I smelled like
Murray's pomade and had
more waves than a "goodbye"
that neither person wants
to happen.

Back then, I would cover
this ocean at night only to
unleash it again in the morning,

hoping someone will notice
the tide and perhaps compliment
the water.

Skin II

When you are the only black man
in the whole neighborhood,

your skin is that one friend who
meets everyone before you do.

It wears a wife beater
and house shoes,

it knocks over the
neighbor's mailbox,

it cusses in front of the kids
and plays the music too loud,

but you actually don't do
any of those things.

It's 7 pm.
It's Wednesday
and you are just

walking home.

Adrenaline Rush

Volcano surfing
is a sport in which a person
rides down an active volcano
at speeds up to 50 miles per hour
using nothing but a wooden board.

When I heard about this activity,
I thought to myself,
it must be nice to feel so safe,
you have to invent new ways to
put yourself in danger.

When the body
thinks it may be swallowing its last breath,
the adrenal glands release hormones into the blood,
the skin becomes a cocktail of sweat and fear,
the heart gets claustrophobic,
the lungs become newlyweds
holding hands in a crashing airplane.
This is called an adrenaline rush.

I was 18 when I started driving.
I was 18 the first time I was pulled over.

It was 2 am on a Saturday.
The officer spilled his lights all over my rearview mirror,
he splashed out of the car with his hand already on his weapon,
and looked at me the way a tsunami looks at a beach house.
Immediately, I could tell he was the kind of man
who brings a gun to a food fight.

He called me son
and I thought to myself,
that's an interesting way of pronouncing "boy."
He asks for my license and registration,
wants to know what I'm doing in this neighborhood,
if the car is stolen,
if I have any drugs
and most days, I know how to grab my voice
by the handle and swing it like a hammer.
But instead,
I picked it up like a shard of glass.
Scared of what might happen if I didn't hold it carefully
because I know that this much melanin
and that uniform is a plotline to a film that
can easily end with a chalk outline baptism,
me trying to make a body bag look stylish for the camera
and becoming the newest coat in a closet full of RIP hashtags.

Once, a friend of a friend asked me
why there aren't more black people in the X Games
and I said, "You don't get it."

Being black is one of the most extreme sports in America.
We don't need to invent new ways of risking our lives
because the old ones have been working for decades.

Jim Crow may have left the nest,
but our streets are still covered with its feathers.
Being black in America is knowing there's a thin line
between a traffic stop and the cemetery,

it's the way my body tenses up
when I hear a police siren in a song,
it's the quiver in my stomach when a cop car is behind me,

it's the sigh of relief when I turn right and he doesn't.
I don't need to go volcano surfing.
Hell, I have an adrenaline rush every time an officer
drives right past without pulling me over

and I realize
I'm going to make it home safe.

This time.

Accent

My mother's accent is
the most popular brand
of salt in her country.

She gently sprinkles a little on
every word before she allows
them to pass her lips.

This is a ceremony that happens
every time she has something to say.

When foreign soil and home
are synonymous, your mouth
becomes a kitchen, each sentence

an entrée. Every time you speak,
you are preparing a meal, the conversation
is a dinner party and you are the chef,

just hoping
that you used
all the correct ingredients.

98

I don't remember the
pledge of allegiance,

but if my iPod plays
"Westside" by TQ,

my fingers will form
a "W" without warning,

my mouth will belt
every word before it
bothers to ask for
my permission,

and suddenly it's 98, R&B
is young and there are still
songs on the radio that can
make you want to love something.

Meal

in a reoccurring
nightmare,

there is
a pack of rabid bullets
smelling one of my
old t-shirts,

hungry
and salivating
at the scent.

they find me with my
hands up, they don't
ask if I'm guilty,

they just eat
until their jaws
are tired
and wipe their
mouths clean when
the meal is over.

Margin

To be marginalized in America
is to be a star on the face of midnight.

We constantly have to rise above everything
and shine our brightest

when it's dark outside.

Liberty

In 1983, illusionist David Copperfield
made the Statue of Liberty disappear.
He placed a curtain in front of the monument
and when he pulled it down the 3,000-foot
statue was no longer there.

I think about how this magic trick
has become too familiar. Liberty
just vanishing without any explanations.

To the Man Standing on the Corner Holding the Sign That Said "God Hates Gays"

I've never seen exactly who it is
that you paperclip your knees,
meld your hands together, and pray to
but I think I know what he looks like:

I bet your God is about 5'10".
I bet he weighs 185. Probably
stands the way a high school
diploma does when it's next to a GED.

I bet your God has a mullet. I bet
he wears flannel shirts with no sleeves,
a fanny pack, and says words like
"getrdun." I bet your God watches FOX news,

Dog the Bounty Hunter, voted for Donald Trump,
and loves Bill O'Reilly. I bet your God
is a politician from Arizona. I bet his
high school served racism in the cafeteria

and offered "hate speech" as a second language.
I bet he has a swastika inside of his throat
and racial slurs tattooed to his tongue
just to make intolerance more comfortable

in his mouth. I bet he has a burning cross
as a middle finger and Jim Crow
underneath his nails. Your God
is a Confederate flag's wet dream.
Conceived on a day when the sky

decided to slice her own wrists.
I bet your God has a drinking problem.
I bet he sees the bottom of the shot glass
more often than his own children.

I bet he pours whiskey on his dreams
until they taste like good ideas,
probably cusses like an electric guitar
with Tourette's plugged into an ocean.

I bet he yells like a schizophrenic nail gun,
damaging all things that care about him
enough to get close. I bet there are angels
in Heaven with black eyes and broken halos

who claimed they fell down the stairs.
I bet your God would've made Eve
without a mouth and taught her how
to spread her legs like a magazine

that she will never ever be pretty enough
to be in. Sooner or later you will realize
that you are praying to your own shadow,
that you are standing in front of mirrors

and are worshipping your own reflection.
Your God stole my God's identity.
So next time you bend your knees,
next time you bow your head

I want you to tell your God
that my God is looking for him.

Brother

When I call
you brother,
it means you have
at least four fists
during any fight
you can't talk
yourself out of.

Sister

When I call you sister.
It means I broke the boy's arm
when he touched you without
your permission.

I'm sorry you had
to see me like that.

Rifle II

On average,
the Mexican government
confiscates approximately
38,000 illegal firearms per year.

After the guns are taken,
they get dismantled
and the metal is used to make
other types of weapons that will
later be utilized by their military.

In 2012,
Pedro Reyes,
an artist from Mexico City,
convinced his government
to donate the guns to him

so he could turn them into
musical instruments.

So somewhere
there is a tambourine
a drum set, a guitar
all made out of things
that were used to take people's lives,
but now they create a sound
that puts life back into people's bodies,
which is to say,
a weapon will always be a weapon
but we choose how we fight the war
and from this I learned that even our most

destructive instruments can still create a melody
worth dancing to
and sometimes isn't that also called a battle?

I wonder how long it took to convince
the first rifle that it could hold a note
instead of a bullet, but still fire into a crowd
and make everyone move.

When I was six,
I was taught how to throw a punch.
In the 80s, that was the anti-bullying movement.

The first time one of my classmates
took a yo mamma joke a little too far,
I remembered all of my training.
I hit the boy in the face,

I turned his nose into a fountain.
My fist was five pennies.

I closed my eyes,
I made a wish,
I came home with bloody knuckles,
and it was the first piece of
artwork we hung on the fridge.

I remember staring at my hands
the same way you stare at a midterm
when all your answers are correct.
I had no idea what class this was
but I did know I was passing
and isn't that what masculinity has become?

A bunch of dudes afraid of their own feelings,
terrified of any emotion other than anger,
yelling at the shadows on the wall,
but still haven't realized
that we're the ones standing in front of the light.

We learn how to dodge a jab,
we learn how to step in before we swing,

we learn that the heart is the same size as the fist,
but we keep forgetting they don't have the same functions.
We keep telling each other to man up
when we don't even know that means.

We turn our boys into bayonets,
point them in the wrong direction,
pull their triggers and fail to acknowledge
all the damage they are doing in the distance.

The word "repurpose"
means to take an object
and give it amnesia.

It means to make something forget what
it's been trained to do so you can
use it for a better reason.

I am learning that this body is not a shotgun.
I am learning that this body is not a pistol.
I am learning that a man is not defined
by what he can destroy.

I am learning that a person
who only knows how to fight
can only communicate in violence
and that shouldn't be anyone's first language.

I am learning that the difference between
a garden and a graveyard is only what
you choose to put in the ground.

One day,
I came across a picture of a strange-looking violin.
The caption said it was made out of a rifle
and I was like,

someday
that can be me.

Simeona

My mother
wears her wrinkles
the way an ocean
wears a wave.

She is the only
body of water

that refuses
to let me drown.

In the Voice of Hip Hop

My father was a motley of sound, a funk band
with bottomless drums and songs that knew nothing

of fatigue. My father had teeth like piano keys, a trumpet
in his spine. He coughed like an old record player

and it sounded like music, but what do I know?
I'm just two turntables and a mic. A sample of a man

I can hardly recognize, a photocopy of an instrument
my fingers never learned how to play and all I know is that

there is an epic sleeping underneath my tongue and I have
a story worth telling so here I am, pouring the containers

that I keep behind my eyes with plans to baptize you
in all the things I've seen. Hoping these words will be the

fire hydrant on your street corner and you will run
through my stories like sprinklers on days when God

plugs in the sun and decides to crank the volume all the way up.

I Bet the Trees Are Thinking

If they're willing to pay
three dollars a gallon for gas,
imagine how much we can
charge them for oxygen.

Roulette

In one of my earliest memories,
I am eight years old,
I have a fistful of afternoon,
and I am asking the summer
if it will always be this glorious.

I remember taking a deep breath.
Trying to get as much July into my lungs
as humanly possible and thinking maybe
I'd be able to convince it that 31 days just isn't enough.

In my neighborhood,
owning a Slip 'N Slide made you a royal family.

In my neighborhood,
we'd fill up our Super Soakers,
shoot each other for hours
And if you didn't have one you
were just a target.

In my neighborhood,
we'd run through sprinklers
like someone who wasn't the boss of us said we couldn't.
Back then the water seemed endless.

Like it didn't have limits
and corners and edges,
like no matter where we were,
if we called out for water,
it would always come running.

When I was a kid,
dragons and droughts
were two things I read about in books,
but never thought I'd actually have to deal with.

I was born and raised in California.
And here, our models and rivers
look like they're on the same diet.
Throughout the years,
I've watched both get smaller and now
I can see their ribs when they exhale.

In California,
our freeways are decorated with signs
that ask us to be careful about how
we use the water.

They hang like an eviction notice
from the environment. I wonder
how long it will take the planet
to tell us we can't live here
and the locks are changed.

I wonder how long it'll be before
my shower becomes a relic,
before my sink tries to change occupations,
before the knobs on my faucet become
roulette wheels, before my hands rain dance
around the spout, hoping a drop will spill from
its neck. I wonder if the next generation
will know water the way I did.

The way it runs through the fingers,
the way it wrinkles the hands,
cools the skin, the way it freezes,
flakes and kisses the ground
on the cheek.

I wonder if my grandkids will
ever throw a penny in a fountain

and hear it splash.

Mercy

after Nikki Giovanni

She asks me to kill the spider.
Instead, I get the most
peaceful weapons I can find.

I take a cup and a napkin.
I catch the spider, put it outside
and allow it to walk away.

If I am ever caught in the wrong place
at the wrong time, just being alive
and not bothering anyone,

I hope I am greeted
with the same kind
of mercy.

IV

Forgiveness

is the well that all of my water
comes from.

I pour it over my past, apologize
to my reflection.

He accepts.

Capacity

Today, I'm trying to perfect the art
of enjoying my own company.

I am exercising isolation
and letting it flex in front
of the mirror like my
proudest muscle.

Some days, it's just me
by myself, the room
is at capacity

and there is nothing
more enticing than silence.

Strength

I convinced my fist
that it was a flower.

I relaxed, it bloomed
and I forgave you before
you even apologized.

Cookout

Somewhere someone's uncle or father,
a man wearing sandals and khaki shorts
who says "back in my day" far too often,

is on the grill. He is watching the food
like he's afraid it'll change its mind
about being a meal and decide to run off

when no one's looking. The kids are playing
a game that they made up themselves
and changing the rules every five minutes.

Their smiles are so big, you can fit history
inside of them and still have room for right
now and the future.

The adults hate all the new music,
but still want the teenagers
to teach them the dances. The Cupid Shuffle

is common ground and the wobble
is a peace treaty signed by both generations.
There are no rallies today, no blood

on this street, no hashtags here, but there is
barbecue, potato salad and greens. The only
tears you will see

is when someone lifts the foil
and all the mac and cheese is finished.

Welcome

So I've never caught a live grenade
with my bare hands.

So I don't know exactly how it feels,
but I imagine it's a lot like getting a text
that says, "Hey, we really need to talk."

The last time I received one of these
messages, I called immediately

and she said,
"I'm going into labor."

My initial thought was,
I don't know much about unions,
but that seems like a good idea.

Before I could actually say that,
she continues with,
"I know I should've told you sooner
...we're having a baby.
Can you come to the hospital?"

And this is how I found out
I was becoming a father.

Most men have nine months to get ready
for something like this, but I had
about nine hours.

I tried to smile in my first family photo,
but complete shock was still the only
outfit my face could squeeze into.

After the picture was taken. I looked down
at my little girl and I said,

"Welcome to the family. Wow.
You sure know how to make an entrance."

Silence

I'm learning
that I don't always
have to make noise
to be seen,

that even my silence
has a spine, a rumble

and says, *I'm here*
in its native tongue.

Complainers

On May 26th, 2003,
Aaron Ralston was hiking,
a boulder fell on his right hand,
he waited four days,
he then amputated
his own arm with a pocketknife.

On New Year's Eve,
a woman was bungee jumping,
the cord broke,
she fell into a river
and had to swim back to land
in crocodile-infested waters
with a broken collarbone.

Claire Champlin was smashed in the face
by a five-pound watermelon
being propelled by a slingshot.

Mathew Brobst was hit by a javelin.

David Striegl was actually
punched in the mouth by a kangaroo.

The most amazing part of these stories
is when asked about the experience
they all smiled, shrugged and said
"I guess things could've been worse."

So go ahead,
tell me you're having a bad day.

Tell me about the traffic.
Tell me about your boss.
Tell me about the job
you've been trying to quit for the past four years.
Tell me the morning is
just a townhouse burning to the ground
and the snooze button is a fire extinguisher.

Tell me the alarm clock
stole the keys to your smile,
drove it into 7 am
and the crash totaled your happiness.
Tell me.
Tell me how blessed are we to have tragedy
so small it can fit on the tips of our tongues.

When Evan lost his legs he was speechless.
When my cousin was assaulted
she didn't speak for 48 hours.
When my uncle was murdered,
we had to send out a search party
to find my father's voice.

Most people have no idea
that tragedy and silence
often have the exact same address.

When your day is a museum of disappointments,
hanging from events that were outside of your control,
when you feel like your guardian
angel put in his two weeks notice two months ago
and just decided not to tell you,
when it seems like God

is just a babysitter that's always on the phone,
when you get punched in the esophagus
by a fistful of life.

Remember,
every year
two million people die of dehydration.
So it doesn't matter if
the glass is half full or half empty.
There's water in the cup.
Drink it and stop complaining.

Muscle is created by lifting things
that are designed to weigh us down.
When your shoulders are heavy
stand up straight and call it exercise.
Life is a gym membership
with a really complicated cancellation policy.

Remember,
you will survive,
things could be worse,
and we are never given
anything we can't handle.
When the whole world crumbles,
you have to build a new one
out of all the pieces that are still here.

Remember,
you are still here.

The human heart beats
approximately 4,000 times per hour
and each pulse,

each throb,
each palpitation is a trophy,
engraved with the words
"You are still alive."
You are still alive.
So act like it.

Yes

And sometimes
it all arrives at once.

The anxiety, the fear,
the voices that scratch
your confidence like
a chalkboard and somehow
all the oxygen in the room
suddenly becomes water
and you begin to wonder if
you have what it takes
to grow gills. You wonder
if you can blend in with the fish.
You wonder if you
will ever breathe again.

And the answer is
not every building that shakes
will collapse.

The answer is
not everything that chips
will crumble.

The answer is
this is temporary
and yes, you will.

Acknowledgments

If I took the time to thank and acknowledge everyone who has influenced, inspired, mentored and/or supported me, this section would be longer than the actual book. With that said, I will do the best to make this both thorough and concise.

Thank you to my family. My parents, Samuel and Simeona, my siblings, Uwani and Lasalle, my Uncle Pine & Aunt Yolly, my cousins Rassan and Jameel. Thank you to the Michael family—Michael, Saba, Degol, Maezn, Ghebriel, and the mother of my daughter, Samra.

Thank you to my poetry family.

Collective Purpose: Jessica Molina, Anthony Blacksher, Thali, Viet Mai, Kendrick Dial and Chris Wilson. You all believed in me well before I believed in myself.

Da Poetry Lounge: Shihan Van Clef and Javon Johnson. You both became my big brothers and challenged me to become better than I thought I could be. I use you both as a measuring sticks and I am honored to have you two as my mentors.

Thank you to Imani Cezanne and Terisa Siagatonu. I love you both dearly. You are phenomenal writers and all-around amazing people.

Krystal and Eric Fountain. You two are probably the only people who've seen my entire progression. You have been supporting me since day one and I can't thank you enough for that.

Thank you to my daughter, Zoey. She doesn't know it yet, but she's teaching me so much about life. I can't wait to return the favor.

Last but not least, thank you to Button Poetry for this amazing opportunity.

About the Author

Rudy Francisco is one of the most recognizable names in Spoken Word Poetry. He was born, raised and still resides in San Diego, California. At the age of 21, Rudy completed his B.A. in Psychology and decided to continue his education by pursuing a M.A. in Organizational Studies. As an artist, Rudy Francisco is an amalgamation of social critique, introspection, honesty and humor. He uses personal narratives to discuss the politics of race, class, gender and religion while simultaneously pinpointing and reinforcing the interconnected nature of human existence.

Other Books by Button Poetry

If you enjoyed this book, please consider checking out some of our others, below. Readers like you allow us to keep broadcasting and publishing. Thank you!

Aziza Barnes, *me Aunt Jemima and the nailgun.*

J. Scott Brownlee, *Highway or Belief*

Nate Marshall, *Blood Percussion*

Sam Sax, *A Guide to Undressing Your Monsters*

Mahogany L. Browne, *smudge*

Neil Hilborn, *Our Numbered Days*

Sierra DeMulder, *We Slept Here*

Danez Smith, *black movie*

Cameron Awkward-Rich, *Transit*

Jacqui Germain, *When the Ghosts Come Ashore*

Hanif Willis-Abdurraqib, *The Crown Ain't Worth Much*

Aaron Coleman, *St. Trigger*

Olivia Gatwood, *New American Best Friend*

Donte Collins, *Autopsy*

Melissa Lozada-Oliva, *Peluda*

William Evans, *Still Can't Do My Daughter's Hair*

Available at buttonpoetry.com/shop and more!